# CONTENTS

## SOURCES

C.M. Offray & Son, Inc.
Rt. 24, Box 601
Chester, NJ 07930
(908) 879-4700
www.offray.com

Wilton Industries
2240 W. 75th St.
Woodridge, IL 60517
(630) 963-1818
(800) 794-5866
www.wilton.com



Production Team: Designer – Patti Sowers; Editorial Writer – Susan McManus Johnson; Technical Writers – Beth Knife and Laura Siar Holyfield; Graphic Designer – Dale T. Rowett; Production Artist – Teresa Boyd; Photography Stylist – Cassie Newsome; Photography – Mark Mathews of Peerless Photography and Don Fraser; Staff Photographer – Russ Ganser

Your wedding will be memorable for many reasons — the love you share with your chosen partner, the good wishes of friends and family, and lots of happy tears and warm laughter, just to name a few. Personalize this special occasion with decorations you've created yourself.

These full-color photographs and easy-to-follow instructions will guide you in making center loop, tie, classic, and floral style bows using sheer and satin ribbons. We've also included four pages of combination bows to show how beautifully these creations work together. For splendid ideas on how to unite your bows with silk flowers, tulle, and lace, turn to page 17.

## MEASURING RIBBON ACCURATELY

Your bow will look its best when you accurately measure the ribbon to make consistent loop sizes and streamer lengths. There are two ways to measure. Follow the method that works best for you or the ribbon you are using.

"Measure and Mark" method. This method can be used for most bows. The first measurement in each bow instruction is for the streamer; the second measurement is for the loop length. Use the ruler below and lightly mark the measurements on the ribbon with a lead pencil before you begin to tie the bow (see a).

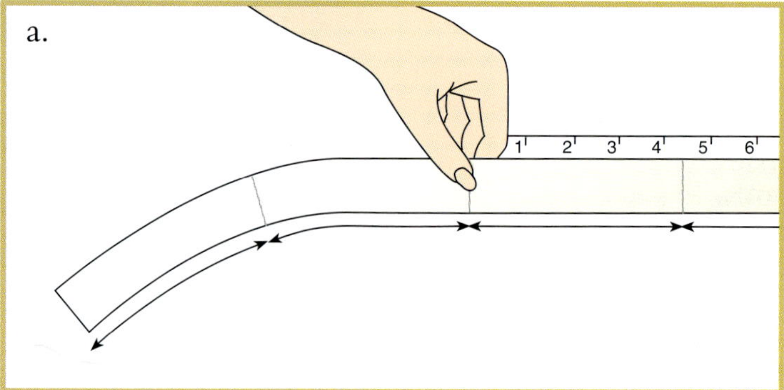


"Measure as You Tie" Method. Use this method for ribbons that cannot be marked or if you do not wish to mark on your ribbon. Use the ruler below to measure the correct length as you form each loop or streamer (see b).

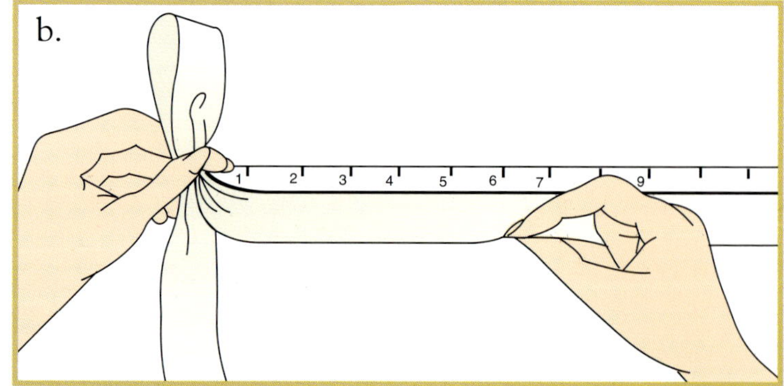

1 2 3 4 5 6 7

## SECURING THE BOW

1. Place a length of wire across center of bow (see c). Bring wire ends to back of bow.

c.

2. Pull loops and streamers forward, away from wire ends. Place index finger between wire ends and against center back of bow; hold wire ends in palm of hand (see d).

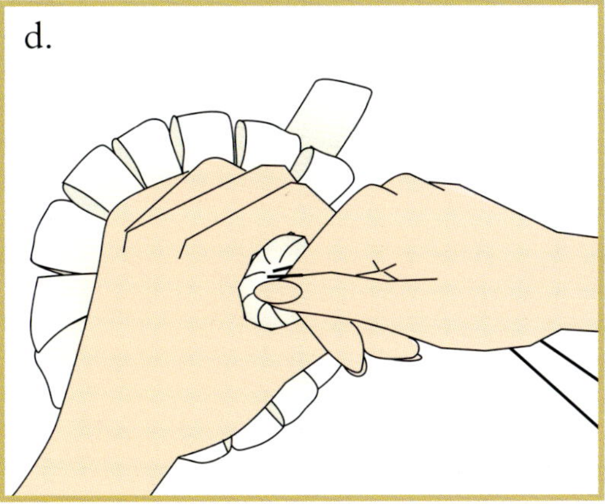
d.

3. Twist bow to tighten wire around center of bow (see e).

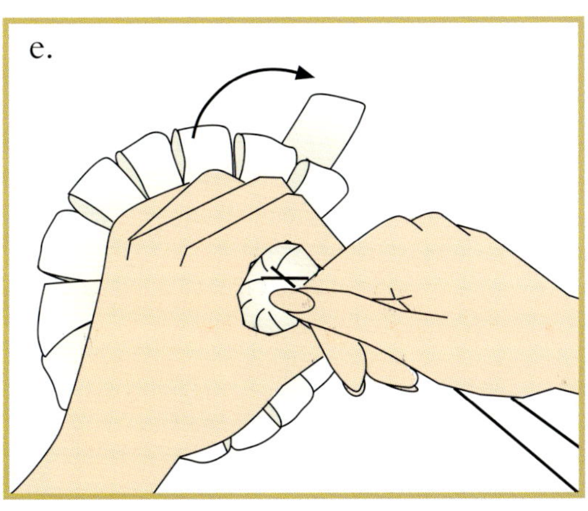
e.

## TRIMMING STREAMERS

Streamers may be trimmed in a variety of ways including angled, straight across, pointed, or notched. To notch or point a streamer end, fold the streamer in half lengthwise and cut at an angle from the folded edge to the open edge.

# The Classic Bow

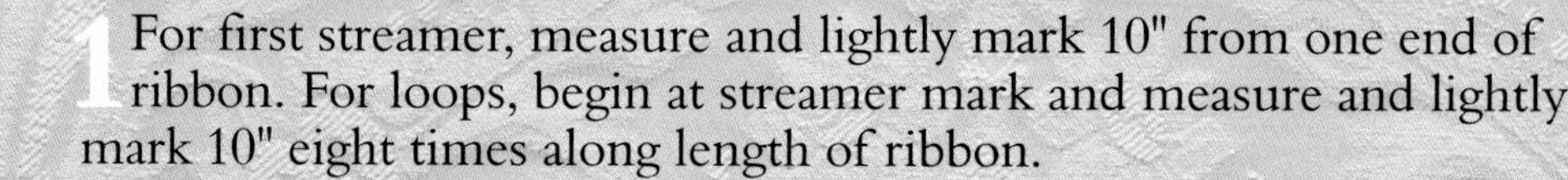

1 For first streamer, measure and lightly mark 10" from one end of ribbon. For loops, begin at streamer mark and measure and lightly mark 10" eight times along length of ribbon.

2 To form first loop, place streamer mark next to first loop mark; gather ribbon between thumb and forefinger (see a).

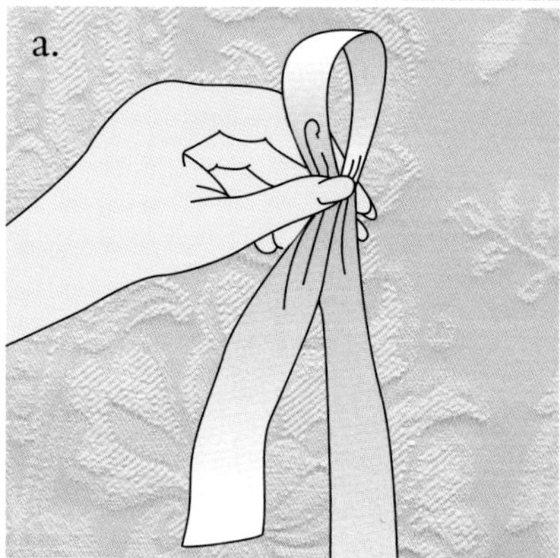

a.

3 To form second loop, place second loop mark next to gathered center (see b); gather ribbon between thumbs and forefingers.

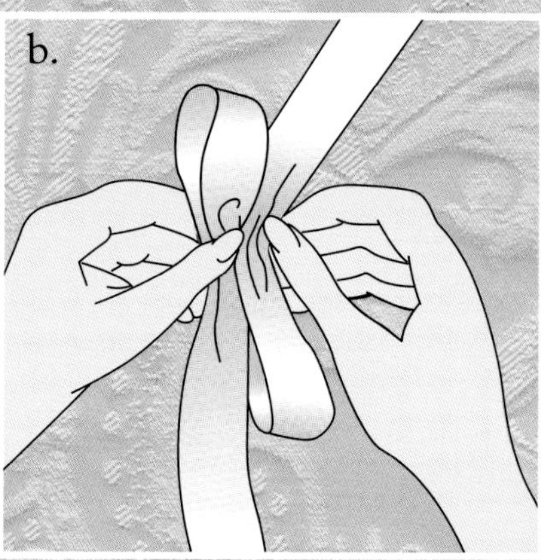

b.

FOR THE 9" DIA. BOW, YOU WILL NEED ONE 3-YD ROLL OF 2½" W WIRE-EDGED RIBBON.

4 Continue placing loop marks next to gathered center, forming loops on alternate sides of gathered center. Complete eight loops.

5 Use wire to secure bow. For second streamer, trim ribbon to 10". Trim streamers and arrange loops.

FOR THE 7" DIA. BOW, YOU WILL NEED ONE 3-YD ROLL OF $1\frac{3}{8}$"W WIRE-EDGED RIBBON.

Follow Steps 1-5, making 10" streamers and eight 8" loops.

FOR THE 5" DIA. BOW, YOU WILL NEED ONE 3-YD ROLL OF $\frac{7}{8}$"W WIRE-EDGED RIBBON.

Follow Steps 1-5, making 10" streamers and eight 6" loops.

**TIP**

**The more bows you make, the easier the bow making will become and the better your bows will look.**

# The Floral Bow

1 For top layer of loops, measure and lightly mark 8" from one end of ribbon for first streamer. For loops, begin at streamer mark and measure and lightly mark 10" eight times along length of ribbon.

2 Hold ribbon at streamer mark, gathering between thumb and forefinger. Twist remaining ribbon one full turn (see a).

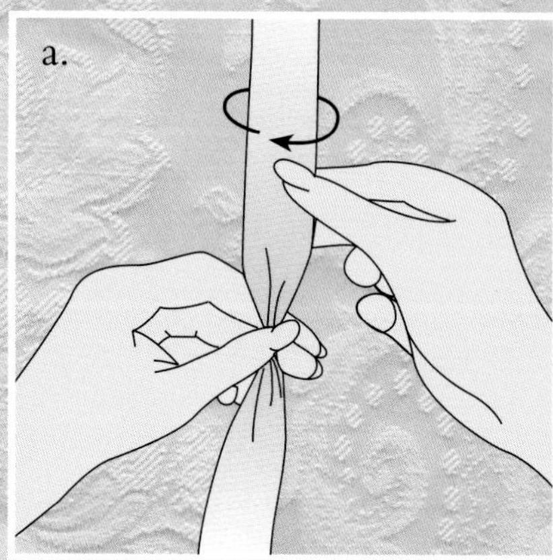


FOR THE 10" DIA. BOW, YOU WILL NEED TWO 3-YD ROLLS OF 2½"W WIRE-EDGED RIBBON.

**TIP**
**Floral and Classic Bows have a similar look. Try both styles to find your favorite method.**

**3** To form first loop, place first loop mark behind streamer mark; gather ribbon between thumb and forefinger. Twist remaining ribbon one full turn (see b).

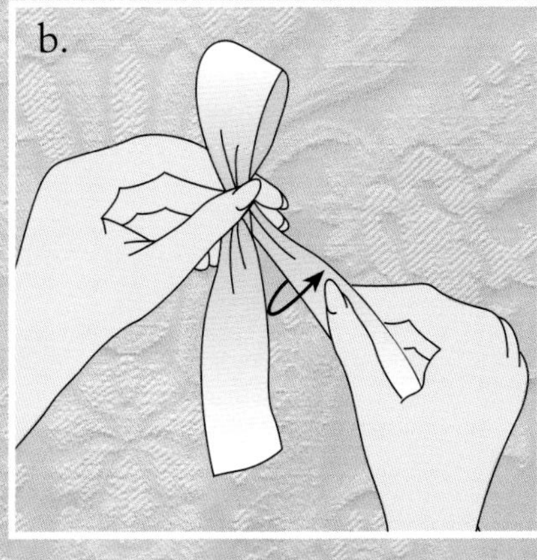


**4** To form second loop, place second loop mark behind first loop mark; gather ribbon between thumb and forefinger. Twist remaining ribbon one full turn (see c).

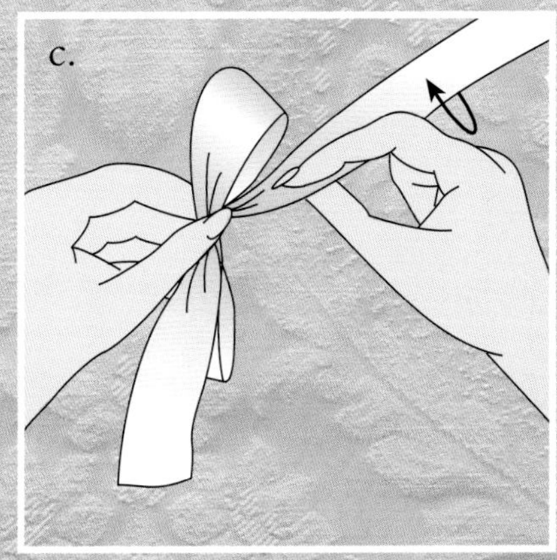


**5** Continue placing loop marks behind previous loop marks and twisting remaining ribbon. Complete eight loops. Use wire to secure top layer of loops. For second streamer, trim ribbon to 8". Trim ribbon ends; set aside.

FOR THE 8" DIA. BOW, YOU WILL NEED ONE 3-YD ROLL OF 2½"W WIRE-EDGED RIBBON.

Follow Steps 1-5, making only one layer of loops with 10" streamers and eight 9" loops.

**6** For bottom layer of loops, measure and lightly mark 12" from one end of second roll of ribbon for first streamer. For loops, begin at streamer mark and measure and lightly mark 12" six times along length of ribbon. Follow steps 2-5, making 12" streamers and six 12" loops. Wire top layer of loops to bottom layer. Trim streamers and arrange loops.

FOR THE 6½" DIA. BOW, YOU WILL NEED ONE 3-YD ROLL OF 1½"W WIRE-EDGED RIBBON.

Follow Steps 1-5, making only one layer of loops with 8" streamers and ten 8" loops.

FOR THE 10" DIA. STACKED TIE BOW, YOU WILL NEED ONE 3-YD ROLL OF 2½"W WIRE-EDGED RIBBON, SILK FLOWER, AND A HOT GLUE GUN.

**1** For first streamer, measure and lightly mark 10" from one end of ribbon. For loops, begin at streamer mark and measure and lightly mark 9" two times, then 11" two times along length of ribbon.

**2** To form first loop, place streamer mark next to first loop mark; gather ribbon between thumb and forefinger (see a).

**3** To form second loop, place second mark next to gathered center; gather ribbon between thumbs and forefingers (see b).

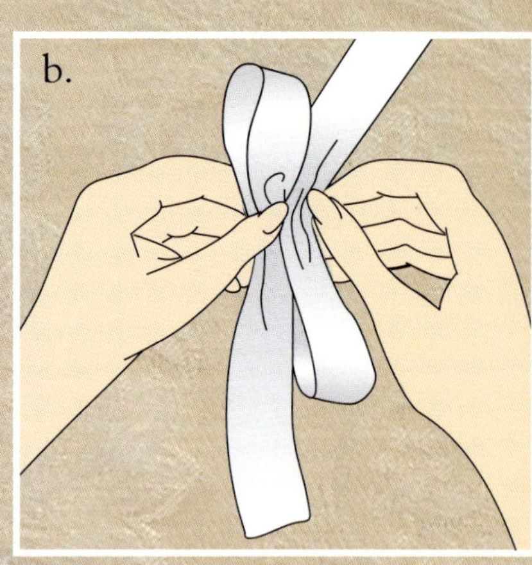


**4** While holding first and second loops, place third loop mark behind gathered center, "layering" third loop behind first loop. Gather ribbon between thumbs and forefingers (see c).

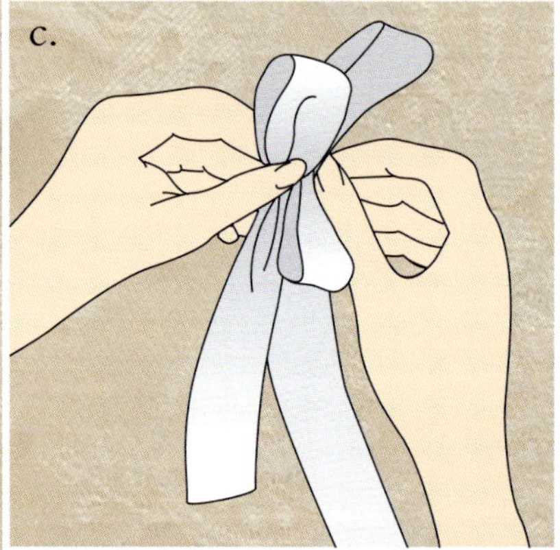


**5** To form fourth loop, repeat Step 4, "layering" fourth loop behind second loop.

**6** Use wire to secure bow. For second streamer, trim ribbon to 10". Trim streamers. Hot glue silk flower to center of bow.

**TIP**

**Before trimming wire ends on a completed bow, consider how the bow will be used. The wire ends are handy for attaching the bow to other projects.**

FOR THE 7" DIA. SHOESTRING TIE BOW, YOU WILL NEED ONE 3-YD ROLL OF 1½"W RIBBON.

1 For first streamer, measure and lightly mark 10" from one end of ribbon. For first loop, begin at streamer mark and measure and lightly mark 8".

2 To form first loop, place first loop mark behind streamer mark; gather ribbon between thumb and forefinger (see a).

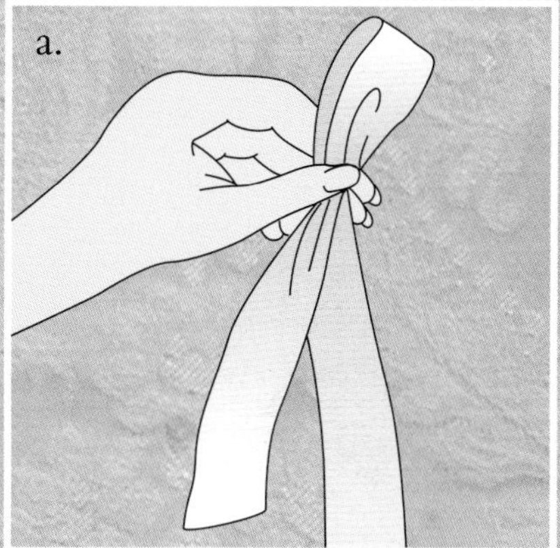
a.

3 Loosely wrap remaining length of ribbon once around thumb (see b). To form second loop, fold remaining ribbon approximately 4" from wrapped area; slide folded end of ribbon through wrapped area.

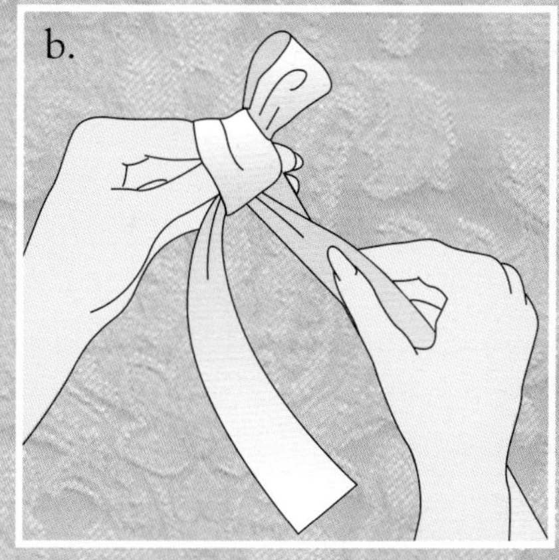
b.

4 Place thumbs inside loops (see c). Pull the loops to tighten bow. Adjust size of loops by pulling on streamers. Trim streamers.

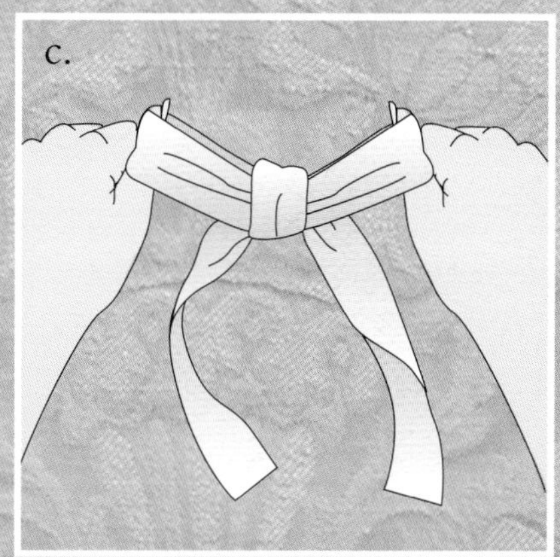
c.

FOR THE 5½" DIA. MULTIPLE RIBBON BOW, YOU WILL NEED 1 YD EACH OF DIFFERENT WIDTHS OF SATIN AND SHEER RIBBONS. (We used five ⅞" – ⅛"w lengths.)

For the Multiple Ribbon Bow, hold all ribbon lengths together (with the widest on the bottom and the most narrow on top) and follow the Shoestring Tie Bow instructions. Tie a length of one remaining ribbon around center of bow over a length of wire; tighten knot.

# The Center Loop Bows

FOR THE 8" DIA. CENTER LOOP FLORAL BOW, YOU WILL NEED ONE 3-YD ROLL OF 2½"W WIRE-EDGED RIBBON.

1 For first streamer, measure and lightly mark 8" from one end of ribbon. For center loop, begin at streamer mark and measure and lightly mark 7". For loops, begin at center loop mark and measure and lightly mark 9" eight times along length of ribbon.

2 Hold ribbon at streamer mark, gathering between thumb and forefinger. Twist remaining ribbon one full turn (see a).

3 To form center loop, place center loop mark behind streamer mark; gather ribbon between thumb and forefinger. Twist remaining ribbon one full turn (see b).

4 To form first loop, place first loop mark behind center loop mark; gather ribbon between thumbs and forefingers (see c). Twist remaining ribbon one full turn.

5 To form second loop, place second loop mark behind first loop mark; gather ribbon between thumbs and forefingers (see d). Twist remaining ribbon one full turn .

6 Continue placing loop marks behind previous loop marks and twisting remaining ribbon. Complete eight loops.

7 Use wire to secure bow. For second streamer, trim ribbon to 8". Trim streamers and arrange loops.

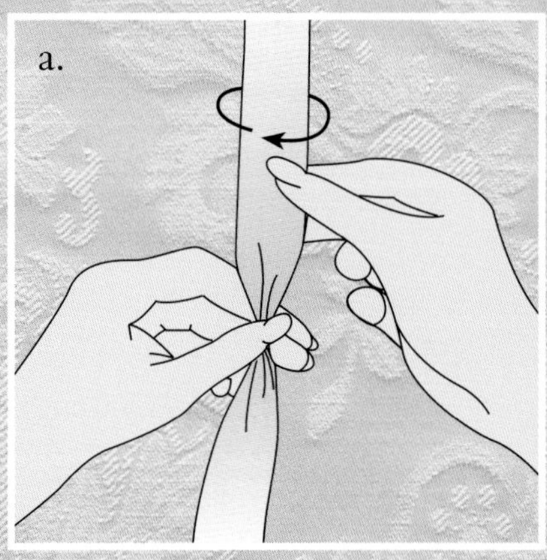

a.

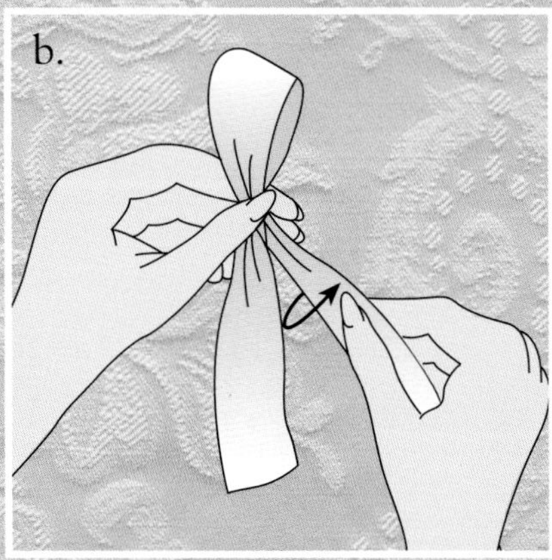

b.

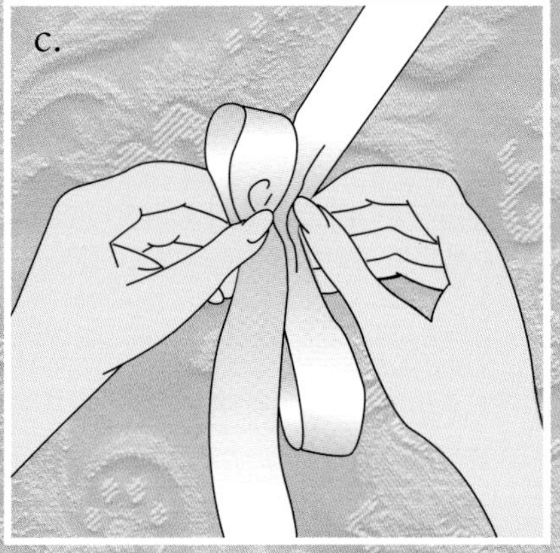

c.

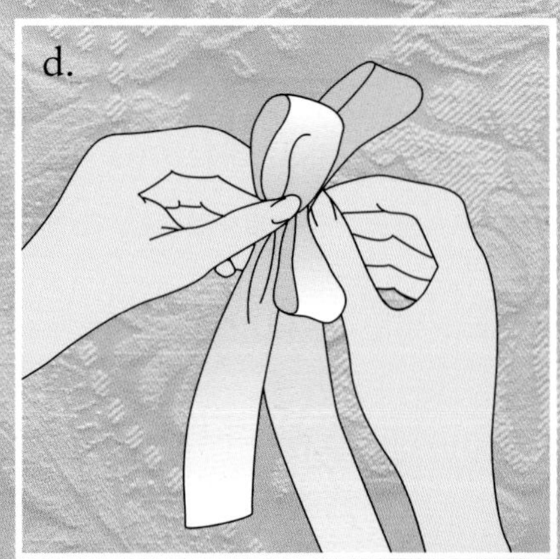

d.

FOR THE 7" DIA. CENTER LOOP CLASSIC BOW, YOU WILL NEED ONE 3-YD ROLL OF 1$^3/_8$"W WIRE-EDGED RIBBON.

FOR THE 7$^1/_2$" DIA. CENTER LOOP TIE BOW, YOU WILL NEED ONE 3-YD ROLL OF 1$^1/_2$"W RIBBON.

1 For first streamer, measure and lightly mark 11" from one end of ribbon. For center loop, begin at streamer mark and measure and lightly mark 4$^1/_2$". For loops, begin at center loop mark and measure and lightly mark 6$^1/_2$" two times, then 8$^1/_2$" two times along length of ribbon.

2 To form center loop, place streamer mark next to center loop mark; gather ribbon between thumb and forefinger (see b). Do not twist ribbon.

3 To form first loop, place first loop mark next to center loop mark; gather ribbon between thumbs and forefingers (see c). Repeat to form second loop.

4 While holding center, first, and second loops, place third loop mark behind gathered center, "layering" third loop behind first loop. Gather ribbon between thumbs and forefingers. Repeat to form fourth loop, "layering" fourth loop behind second loop.

5 Use wire to secure bow. For second streamer, trim ribbon to 11". Trim streamers and arrange loops.

1 For first streamer, measure and lightly mark 10" from one end of ribbon. For center loop, begin at streamer mark and measure and lightly mark 4$^1/_2$". For loops, begin at center loop mark and measure and lightly mark 8" six times along length of ribbon.

2 To form center loop, place streamer mark next to center loop mark; gather ribbon between thumb and forefinger (see b). Do not twist ribbon.

3 To form first loop, place first loop mark next to center loop mark (see c). Gather ribbon between thumbs and forefingers.

4 Continue placing loop marks next to gathered center, forming loops on alternate sides of gathered center. Complete six loops.

5 Use wire to secure bow. For second streamer, trim ribbon to 10". Trim streamers and arrange loops.

FOR THE
7" DIA.
SHEER BOW
WITH SATIN
CENTER BOW,
YOU WILL NEED
ONE 3-YD ROLL
OF $1^3/_8$"W SHEER
WIRE-EDGED
RIBBON AND
ONE 3-YD ROLL
OF $^5/_8$"W SATIN
WIRE-EDGED RIBBON.

Follow the Classic Bow instructions, page 5, making sheer bow with 11" streamers and eight 8" loops and satin bow with 11" streamers and eight 6" loops. Wire satin bow to center of sheer bow.

**Tip**

**To determine the amount of ribbon you will need for any size bow, follow this guide:**

Add 1" to diameter you want the finished bow to be:

________ in.

Multiply this measure by the number of loops you want:

x________

Add the length, in inches, of streamers (if any):

+________ in.

Add the length, in inches, of center loop (if any):

+________ in.

Divide by 36 to get the total ribbon yardage needed:

________ yds.

# The Combination Bows

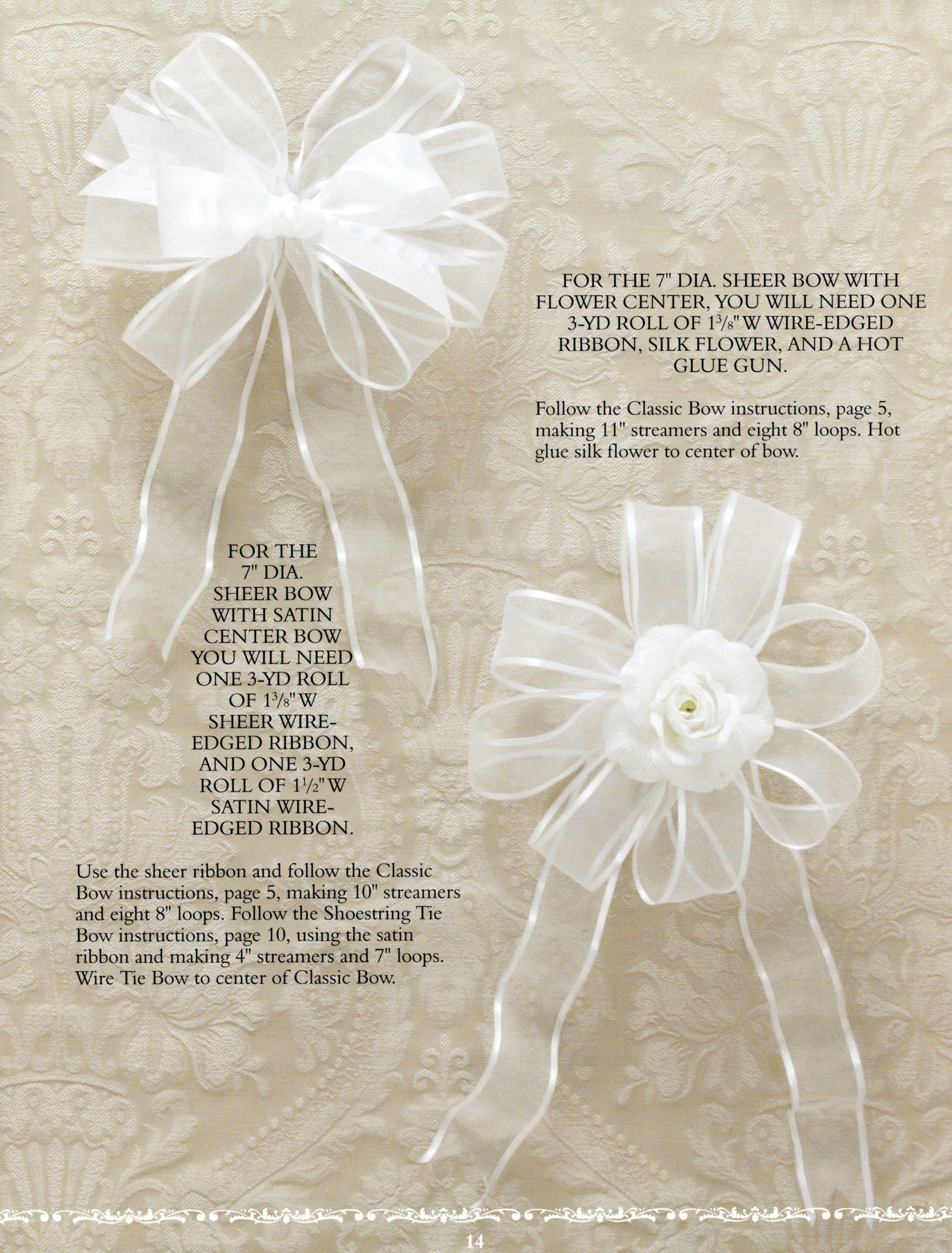

FOR THE 7" DIA. SHEER BOW WITH FLOWER CENTER, YOU WILL NEED ONE 3-YD ROLL OF 1$^{3}/_{8}$"W WIRE-EDGED RIBBON, SILK FLOWER, AND A HOT GLUE GUN.

Follow the Classic Bow instructions, page 5, making 11" streamers and eight 8" loops. Hot glue silk flower to center of bow.

FOR THE 7" DIA. SHEER BOW WITH SATIN CENTER BOW YOU WILL NEED ONE 3-YD ROLL OF 1$^{3}/_{8}$"W SHEER WIRE-EDGED RIBBON, AND ONE 3-YD ROLL OF 1$^{1}/_{2}$"W SATIN WIRE-EDGED RIBBON.

Use the sheer ribbon and follow the Classic Bow instructions, page 5, making 10" streamers and eight 8" loops. Follow the Shoestring Tie Bow instructions, page 10, using the satin ribbon and making 4" streamers and 7" loops. Wire Tie Bow to center of Classic Bow.

FOR THE
11" DIA.
SHEER BOW
WITH SATIN
CENTER BOW,
YOU WILL NEED
ONE 3-YD ROLL OF
$2^1/_2$" W SHEER WIRE-EDGED RIBBON AND
ONE 3-YD ROLL OF $1^1/_2$" W
SATIN WIRE-EDGED RIBBON.

Use the sheer ribbon and follow the Classic Bow instructions, page 5, making 11" streamers and four 12" loops. Follow the Shoestring Tie Bow instructions, page 10, using the satin ribbon and making 10" streamers and 9" loops. Tie a length of satin ribbon around center of bows.

**TIP** If you want to re-tie a bow, many ribbons can be pressed or steamed with an iron to remove wrinkles and restore the original finish.

# More Combination Bows

FOR THE 9" DIA. SATIN BOW WITH SHEER CENTER BOW, YOU WILL NEED ONE 3-YD ROLL OF $2^1/_2$"W SATIN WIRE-EDGED RIBBON AND ONE 3-YD ROLL OF $1^1/_2$"W SHEER WIRE-EDGED RIBBON.

Follow the Classic Bow instructions, page 5, using the satin ribbon. Follow Steps 1-5 of the Floral Bow instructions, pages 7 and 8, using sheer ribbon and making 12" streamers and ten 8" loops. Wire sheer bow to center of satin bow.

**TIP**

Buy an extra roll of ribbon if you want extra-long streamers. They can be added after the bow is tied. Wire or hot glue streamers to the back of your bow.

# Aisle Arrangements

*For your wedding procession, line the aisles with blossoms and shining ribbons! Use hand-fashioned bows and silk floral candle rings to create these delights for the eye.*

For true elegance, rely on lilies! This enchanting arrangement makes use of two fluffy bows and a candle ring of silk lilies and gardenias. Begin by making two Tie Bows with 10" loops from tulle ribbon. Use chenille stems to wire these to a pew clip. Cut a 4" diameter floral candle ring in half, saving one of the halves to be used on another pew bow. Wire remaining half-ring to the pew clip, placing it on top of the tulle bow. Using 2$^{1}/_{2}$" wide plaid sheer ribbon, make a Classic Bow with six 10" loops and extra-long streamers. Wire sheer bow to the pew clip beneath the flowers.

***Opposite:*** Breathtaking mini wreaths are amazingly simple to create! Start by wiring a pew clip to the back of a 6$^{1}/_{2}$" diameter floral candle ring. Make a Tie Bow with 2$^{1}/_{2}$" wide ribbon, two 10" loops, and two 8" loops. Attach finished Tie Bow to the candle ring and pew clip with a Tie Bow of 1$^{1}/_{2}$" wide ribbon with two 6" loops.

*In the language of flowers, white roses say "only for thee." Assemble a sweet nosegay to dress the arm of each pew or let a joyous cascade of blooms and shimmering ribbons spill into the aisles.*

To make this romantic pew arrangement, use a chenille stem to wire a plastic pew clip to a small silk floral bush. For the large bow, use 2$^{3}/_{8}$" wide plaid sheer ribbon and make a Classic Bow with four 10" loops. Using six lengths of $^{1}/_{4}$" wide ribbon, make a Tie Bow to attach your sheer bow to the pew clip.

Opposite: For this abundance of blossoms, use a chenille stem to wire a cascading floral stem to a plastic pew clip. Wire two stems of roses — flower ends down — on top of the cascade. Using 2$^{1}/_{2}$" wide iridescent mesh ribbon, make a Center Loop Classic Bow with six 10" loops. Use wire to attach the bow to rose stems at top of cascade.

# Candle HOLDERS

*Solemnize your vows by the glow of wax tapers in elegant candelabras. And you'll forever remember the lighting of your unity candle — it's destined to be a cherished keepsake!*

Dress a large candelabra with a swag of silk bridal flowers, then add depth to your arrangement with a combination bow. Use chenille stems to wire the floral swag to the center of the candelabra. Make a Floral Bow with eight 12" loops using 2½" wide satin ribbon. Make a Classic Bow with eight 10" loops using 2½" wide sheer ribbon. Wire Classic Bow to Floral Bow. Use chenille stems to wire Floral Bow to the candelabra and the floral swag.

Left: Swathe a meaningful pillar in delicate satin and silk — it's easier than it looks. Tie a 1/4" wide ribbon around the base of the candle. Use six lengths of ribbon, ranging from 1/8" to 1 3/8" wide, to make a Tie Bow. Using the ribbon already tied to the candle, tie the bow to the candle. Hot glue a ribbon rose in the center of the bow. Place the candle in a floral candle ring.

Above: Adorning this small candelabra takes just two easy steps. Make a Tie Bow with four 8" loops using 1 1/2" wide ribbon. Use chenille stems to wire a floral bush and the bow to the center of the candelabra.

# CENTERPIECES

There's something very special about this centerpiece — it all begins with a cake stand, turned upside-down! Wrap ivy garland in a circle to fit the cake stand. Cut apart three floral stems of roses and hot glue these to the wreath. Using 2½" wide sheer ribbon, make four Classic Bows with two 8" loops each. Using tulle ribbon, tie the Classic Bows to the wreath. Place a pillar candle in the base of the cake stand.

## *Is it a centerpiece or a clever conversation piece? Let your guests decide.*

This quick arrangement is a small floral bush, flattened with the stems fanning out from the center, and a heart-shaped glass dish. Using 1½" wide ribbon and forming 7" loops, tie a Tie Bow around the dish. Place the dish at the center of the flowers. Fill the dish with faceted beads and three votive-size candles.

Left and opposite left: These appealing topiary "trees" are actually floral bushes. For each topiary base, spray a clay pot with white paint. If you like, sponge the pot with gold paint. Fill the pot with floral foam and tulle. Push all flowers and leaves on a floral bush to top of stems; wire stems together below flowers. Push the newly formed "trunk" into the foam. Knot the center of a 1/4" wide ribbon at the base of the tree. Wrap and crisscross the ribbon ends around the trunk. Tie ribbon ends into a Tie Bow just under flowers. For added fullness, use 7/8" wide ribbon to make a Classic Bow with eight 6" loops. Wire Classic Bow over the Tie Bow. When placing on table, arrange votive cups around your topiary and sprinkle faceted sequins over the tablecloth.

Opposite right, above: This instant tabletop décor is made by tying three tall bud vases together with a Tie Bow of 1 1/2" wide ribbon. Fill vases with tulle pieces and a floral bush cut into separate stems.

Opposite right, below: Let candlelight twinkle from this quick centerpiece! Cut a six-foot floral garland in half. Wire the ends of one half together, forming a ring. Tie ring to a 12" diameter grapevine wreath using four tulle ribbon Tie Bows. Using three ribbons in widths varying from 1/8" to 5/8" for each bow, make Tie Bows to hot glue on the tulle bows. Place a candle base, a pillar candle, and a hurricane chimney in the center of the wreath.

# Door Wreaths

### Tip

*Use an over-the-door hook to hang your wreath in an entryway where wires might scratch the door's finish. If your wreath will beautify a wall, loop a piece of wire on the back of the wreath to hang on a nail — so quick, so easy!*

*When placed on the door, a lacy white wreath announces the joyful event proceeding within.*

To create a cascade of flowers on your wreath, begin by wrapping a ring of grapevine with white tulle ribbon. Wire the ends to the back of the wreath. Flatten a large, cascading floral bush, spreading the flowers to either side of where the bow will go. Wire the bush to the top of the wreath. Wire two stems of roses to each side on top of the floral bush. Make a Tie Bow with two lengths of tulle ribbon and wire the bow to the wreath over the flower stems. Using $2^{3}/_{8}$" wide dotted sheer ribbon, make a Classic Bow with eight 10" loops. Wire Classic Bow to wreath over Tie Bow.

Opposite: A silk ivy swag looks natural when wired to a grapevine wreath. The blooms are a floral candle ring, cut in half and glued to the ivy swag. For the bow, use two yards of 7" wide lace to make a Tie Bow. Wire the Tie Bow in place. Using $2^{1}/_{2}$" wide satin ribbon, make a Center Loop Classic Bow with one 6" center loop and six 10" loops. Wire Center Loop Bow to Tie Bow.

# Cake TOPPERS

*The grand finale to any wedding reception, the bride's cake will draw almost as many eyes as the happy couple themselves. Personalize your cake with a topper of your own creation. There are an abundance of statuettes, mini bouquets, hearts, bells, and other pre-made toppers that you can embellish with bows. Consider leaving long streamers on the bows. These can be trimmed to fit the cake once the topper is in place.*

Above: For this bride-and-groom topper, begin with a 6" diameter doily and a cardboard circle cut slightly smaller. Using 2½" wide ribbon, make a Classic Bow with eight 8" loops and no streamers; hot glue doily to cardboard and bow to doily. Glue figures to bow. Make two more Classic Bows with long streamers: one with 1⅜" wide sheer ribbon and six 8" loops, the other with ⅝" satin ribbon and eight 7" loops. Tuck these bows and a small bouquet of silk flowers with pearl streamers behind the figures, gluing them to the first bow and to the back of figures.

Opposite and right: Make your cake lovely in an instant by wiring a Floral Bow to a purchased cake topper or bouquet. The effect of this simple decoration is breathtaking, but leaves you with plenty of time to prepare for your special day.

# *Please* BE SEATED

*In just a little more time than it takes to tie a bow, any seating can be made to fit your wedding theme!*

Effortless chair-dressing is yours in an instant! Simply fold a cutwork place mat over a chair back. Make one Tie Bow on each side, threading the ribbons through the cutwork to secure the place mat.

Love the airy beauty of lace? Here's a delicate-looking but sturdy way to use lace in your reception or outdoor ceremony. Swathe each chair in a half-yard of 45" wide lace fabric, tying or wiring the ends together at center back of the chair. Make a four-loop Classic Bow. Use 1/8" and 3/16" wide ribbons to tie the bow to the knot of lace. Tuck a stem of silk flowers behind the bow.

The drapable quality of ivy makes it a decorator favorite. This classic greenery is also a traditional symbol of marriage and fidelity. We used one-half of a six-foot ivy garland on this chair back. To do, swag the garland from the top of chair uprights and attach with chenille stems. Using 1 1/2" wide pearl-trimmed ribbon, make two Classic Bows with four 8" loops each. Use a length of tulle to tie each bow to a chair upright.

One definition of "elegance" is "restrained style." We think this charming chair back decoration is the model of refinement. Tie a two-yard length of 7" wide lace trim around the middle of the chair back. Make a four-loop Classic Bow. Use two 1/4" wide ribbons to tie the Classic Bow to the knot of the lace trim.

# Table Dressing

What could be more elegant than flowers falling from a combination bow? To create your own spill of blossoms, begin by making two Classic Bows, one with four 10" loops from 2½" wide iridescent mesh ribbon, the other with four 8" loops from 1½" wide pearl-trimmed ribbon. Wire the smaller bow to larger bow, then wire the combination bow to a silk floral cascade. Hot glue a flower from the cascade to the center of the bows. Wire the finished decoration to a gather in your tablecloth.

## *Tempting tables make your reception a feast for the eye. Use safety pins to gather your tablecloth, then wire your beautiful bows to the pins.*

Right: Gather your tablecloth bunting-style with a rounded Classic Bow and a posy of blooms. To fashion this simple table décor, use $2^{3}/_{8}$" wide sheer ribbon to make a Classic Bow with eight 10" loops. Wire the bow to a small bush of flowers, then wire the flowers to a gather in your tablecloth.

Left: This quick table décor is a purchased rose garland, swagged with Tie Bows and pinned to a tablecloth. For each bow needed, hold together one $1^{1}/_{2}$" wide sheer ribbon and one $1^{1}/_{2}$" wide satin ribbon to make a Tie Bow with 8" loops. To attach bow to garland, tie a $^{1}/_{8}$" wide and a $^{1}/_{4}$" wide ribbon in a Tie Bow around first bow and garland. Gather tablecloth with a safety pin, then wire bows to pin, swagging garland between bows.

# For the Procession

For this tender heart, add bows to the center of a purchased satin pillow. Begin by making a Classic Bow with four 6" loops using 7/8" wide sheer ribbon. Hot glue the bow to the pillow. Make a Tie Bow using one length each of 1/8" and 1/4" wide ribbon, leaving streamers extra-long to secure the rings. Hot glue Tie Bow to Classic Bow. Glue a ribbon rose in the center of the bows.

## *Your ring bearer and flower girl will look adorable carrying these easy-to-make accessories.*

Left: For this flower-ringed basket, you'll need a floral candle ring and a basket with a tall handle. Wrap the handle with tulle ribbon, allowing ends to extend 3" below handle. Tie tulle to handle, using $1^1/_2$" wide ribbon to make Tie Bows with 5" loops. Using $^1/_8$" and $^1/_4$" wide ribbons together, make Tie Bows around handle and large bows. Hot glue candle ring to inside edge of basket, cutting the ring if necessary.

Right: Wrap an 11" high basket with tulle ribbon, gluing the ends below one handle. Wrap $^1/_8$" and $^3/_8$" wide ribbons around the basket's handle, gluing in place near the top edge of basket. Using tulle ribbon, make Tie Bows with 7" loops on each side of handle. Use one length each of $^1/_8$", $^1/_4$", and $1^5/_8$" wide ribbons to make Tie Bows to glue to handle and tulle bows. Cut two silk rosebuds from their stems. Hot glue one rosebud to each combination bow. Line the basket with a doily or piece of lace.

# The Toasting Table

*It's a joyful moment — sharing a toast to the future with your best-beloved while receiving the good wishes of all those near and dear to you. Make your toasting glasses, cake knife, and cake server reflect the radiance of the day.*

Opposite: For each piece of stemware, make a two-loop classic bow using 1 3/8" wide sheer ribbon. To fasten the sheer bows to the glass stems, use 1/4" wide satin ribbon to make Tie Bows with two 2 1/2" loops. A single silk blossom hot glued to the center of each bow salutes the miracle of your love.

Left and above: Use the same romantic floral treatment for your cake knife and cake server as that used on the happy couple's toasting glasses. For each serving piece, tie a piece of tulle around stemware or utensil handle. Using a 5/8" wide wire-edged satin ribbon, make a Tie Bow with two 3" loops. To attach satin bows to serving pieces over tulle, use a 1/4" wide sheer ribbon to make Tie Bows with two 3" loops. Hot glue or wire small roses at center of each bow.

# Little Favors

*Guests will relive the wedding festivities while they enjoy a bag of crunchy snack mix, courtesy of the newlyweds. Or, if you favor candy, paper cones filled with sugary treats will make a sweet presentation for all attendees.*

Opposite: For each snack sack, fill a resealable plastic bag with Favorite-of-the-Bride Snack Mix. Place bag inside a 4½" wide paper sack. Fold the top of the sack several times. Fold a 6" diameter paper doily in half and place over the top of sack. Using a hole punch, make two holes through all folded layers. Thread one length each of cord and 3/16" wide ribbon through the holes, adding a small celebration bell. Tie cord and ribbon into a Tie Bow with 5" loops.

## FAVORITE-OF-THE-BRIDE SNACK MIX

*1 package (12.5 ounces) white yogurt-covered raisins*
*1 package (7.5 ounces) white chocolate-covered pretzels*
*1 cup white chocolate-covered almonds*
*1 cup white gourmet jelly beans*

*In a very large bowl, combine raisins, pretzels, almonds, and jelly beans. Store in an airtight container in a cool place.*

*Yield: about 6 cups snack mix*

Above: To create each candy cone, fold an 8" diameter paper doily in half. Roll doily into a cone shape and hot glue the overlapping edges. For handle, tie a knot in each end of a 12" length of 7/8" wide sheer ribbon. Hot glue knots to cone. Wrap candies in two layers of tulle. Gather and tie the tulle with a 12" length of ribbon or cord, making a Tie Bow. Place wrapped candy in cone.

*Memories are made of this! Gift your guests with attractive favors that are almost too pretty to open. They'll love having mementos of your happy day.*

Right and below: Given these fun favors, wedding attendees will enjoy showering the newlyweds in drifts of iridescent bubbles. Dressing up the bottles couldn't be simpler: Wrap each bottle in layers of tulle. Gather the tulle and secure it with the wire stem of one or more small silk flowers. To cover the wire, tie $^{1}/_{2}$" or $^{1}/_{4}$" wide ribbon into a Tie Bow with 3" loops.

Above: Purchased $2\frac{1}{2}$" high favor boxes in the shape of treasure chests are another quick-to-complete gift for guests. These are especially effective when decorated in your wedding colors! Hot glue the top 2" of a rose stem, including the leaves, to the lid of each filled box. Wrap two lengths of $\frac{1}{8}$" wide ribbon around each box, tying ribbon ends into Tie Bows with 3" loops.

Left: For fast-to-finish favors, use the new "pocket" ribbon available at craft and floral shops. Cut the ribbon near each stitched line and fill the resulting "pockets" with treats. Gather each pocket and use the wire stem of a small silk flower to twist it closed. To cover the wire, tie $\frac{1}{8}$" wide and $\frac{1}{4}$" wide ribbons together into a Tie Bow with 4" loops.

# Bouquets & Boutonnieres

Magnificent to behold, this bouquet is just two purchased floral bridal "bushes" layered together and placed in a cone-shaped bouquet holder. Make whatever bow you wish for your own unique arrangement. We wired a six-loop Classic Bow of $^5/_8$" wide satin ribbon to an eight-loop Classic Bow of $1^1/_2$" wide sheer ribbon, allowing plenty of extra ribbon for the long streamers.

*Choose traditional white lilies, palest orchids, radiant red roses, or deep blue hydrangeas. With the incredible variety of silk blossoms available, no bride has to deny herself the flowers she loves best.*

Below: Make a handsome boutonniere for every gentleman in the wedding party. Trim the stem of a silk rosebud to about 3" long. Wrap the stem with green florist's tape. Tie a 7/8" wide wire-edged ribbon into a Tie Bow with 3" loops around the stem. Use a florist's pin on the back of a lapel to secure stem to lapel.

Above: This arrangement can be carried by the bride or by her attendants. It also makes a fine "toss away" bouquet for the bride to throw at her reception. A purchased silk nosegay like this one is sometimes called a "French bouquet" because the stems are attached to one another and form a handle. To dress it up, wrap and criss-cross two lengths of 5/8" wide ribbon from bottom of handle to just beneath blossoms and leaves, using glue to secure ribbon at top and bottom. Using 1 3/8" wide sheer ribbon, make a four-loop Classic Bow. To attach sheer bow to bouquet, use satin ribbons in widths of 1/8", 1/4", and 5/8" to make a Tie Bow.

# Friends & Family

*Signs of joyful times: Display your engagement photo for all to see, and let pretty reservation cards remove the guesswork at your reception.*

Show the happy couple to best advantage in a bow-bedecked openwork frame. Make a Tie Bow with 7" loops using 2 3/8" wide dotted sheer ribbon. Use 3/4" wide sheer ribbon to make a four-loop Classic Bow; wire this bow to dotted sheer bow. Wire the combined bow to the frame. Glue a flower to the center of the bow.